The Visual Guide t

Asperger's Syndrome (1)

by Alis Rowe

Also by Alis Rowe

One Lonely Mind
978-0-9562693-0-0

The Girl with the Curly Hair - Asperger's and Me
978-0-9562693-2-4

The 1st Comic Book
978-0-9562693-1-7

The 2nd Comic Book
978-0-9562693-4-8

The 3rd Comic Book
978-0-9562693-3-1

The 4th Comic Book
978-15086839-7-1

The 5th Comic Book
978-15309879-3-1

Websites:
www.thegirlwiththecurlyhair.co.uk
www.thecurlyhairconsultancy.com
www.theliftingplace.com

Social Media:
www.facebook.com/thegirlwiththecurlyhair
www.twitter.com/curlyhairedalis

The Visual Guide to

Asperger's Syndrome (1)

by Alis Rowe

Lonely Mind Books
London

For anyone who wants to learn about autism and Asperger's Syndrome

hello

Autism is often described as "a different way of experiencing the world", but this sentence can be really difficult to understand, let alone imagine.

Had someone ever said that phrase to me, I think it would've confused me rather than educated me! I would have thought, "different in what way?" and "different, how?"

So in this book I have tried to cover the fundamentals of autism so that by the time you have finished, you will have a clearer idea of what autism actually is and how it is likely to affect someone.

Always remember that everyone is different, but hopefully this guide will give you a good foundation in understanding autism which can be adapted for yourself or for the individual you know.

Alis aka The Girl with the Curly Hair

Contents

Note:

In order to make things clear, The Girl with the Curly Hair has differentiated between autistic people and non-autistic people using the colours blue and green

Blue represents autistic
Green represents non-autistic

She refers to non-autistic people as neurotypical (NT) people

The terms and colours are not intended to be derogatory in any way, The Girl with the Curly Hair uses them to make her resources clear and easy to follow

What is ASD?

ASD stands for Autism Spectrum Disorder

At the time of writing, this is the name most commonly used for a range of similar conditions, including Asperger's Syndrome

ASD is a lifelong developmental condition that affects the way a person experiences the world

It means a person has persistent difficulties in two main areas of life - their relationships with other people, and how they cope with the environment around them

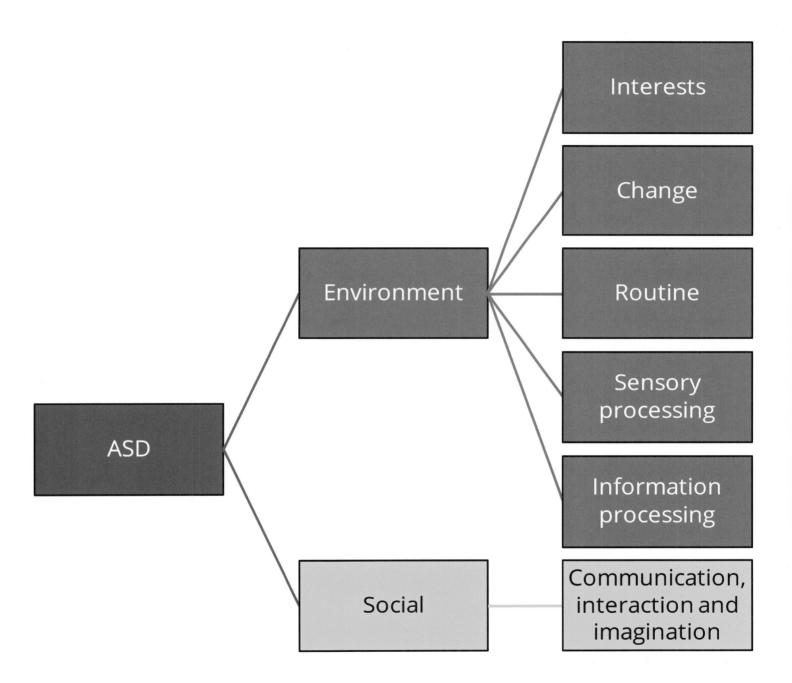

There are currently many different names used when talking about ASD, which can be confusing. Generally they all mean the same thing...

The words and terms an autistic person uses to describe themselves is normally a personal choice

Some autistic people have strong preferences on what their condition should be called, some autistic people like The Girl with the Curly Hair won't give a second thought to it!

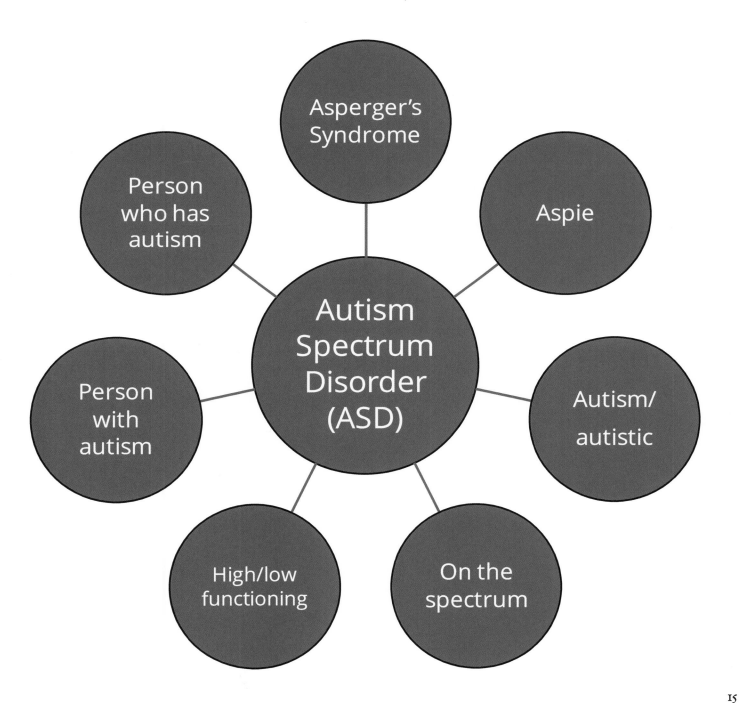

Some autistic people also feel uncomfortable about the word 'disorder', preferring to call it a 'condition' instead

Some autistic people don't consider their ASD to be a 'disability', they consider it to be a 'difference'

The Girl with the Curly Hair doesn't have any particular preference on the words and language that are used, but in her work she primarily uses the term 'ASD', simply because that's what is most commonly used and recognised in the UK at the moment

In order to have ASD, an individual must have persistent difficulties with social interaction (often broken down into social communication, social interaction and social imagination):

Social interaction – having uncommon interests, having unusual preferences for ways of interacting with people

Social communication – having problems with body language, tone of voice, spoken word, etc.

Social imagination – having trouble understanding other people's thoughts and feelings, and predicting consequences

ASD socialising areas of difficulty

Here's an example of The Boy with the Spiky Hair having some social difficulties at football club...

In addition, an individual must also have persistent difficulties with their environment:

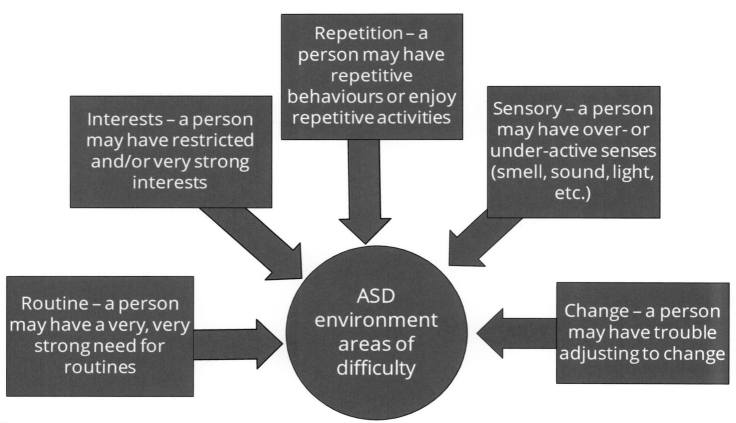

Repetition – a person may have repetitive behaviours or enjoy repetitive activities

Interests – a person may have restricted and/or very strong interests

Sensory – a person may have over- or under-active senses (smell, sound, light, etc.)

Routine – a person may have a very, very strong need for routines

ASD environment areas of difficulty

Change – a person may have trouble adjusting to change

A 'routine' is not limited to simply being the way an individual structures their day. The table below gives some other examples of types of routine:

Type of routine	Examples from The Girl with the Curly Hair
A desire to have and maintain sameness	She only wants to eat the same brand of corn flakes; she likes every day to be exactly the same
The order in which tasks are done	She likes to do her newspaper rounds, then eat breakfast, and then walk the dog
The method by which a task is done	She has a particular way of preparing her meals, for example her idea of a 'sandwich' is bread on one side of the plate and the filling on the other side
The time that a task or activity is done	She likes to lift weights at exactly 9.00a.m.; she likes to eat dinner at exactly 5.00p.m.
The structure and plan of the day as a whole	Every day she has plans to do her newspaper rounds, walk the dog, do weightlifting and do her work all at particular times

Some autistic people have no structure to their days at all, but still rely on routines

At the time of writing, it's thought that approximately 1 in 100 people in the UK have ASD*

Less is known about ASD in women and girls. Current ratios suggest that more males have ASD. Statistics range from 2:1 to 16:1 males:females*

* National Autistic Society. 2018. Autism facts and history. [ONLINE] Available at: https://www.autism.org.uk/about/what-is/myths-facts-stats. aspx [Accessed 11 August 2018].

There are some problems with these statistics however:

The main one is that ASD is a hidden condition – you can't always tell if someone has ASD

There's no single definitive test for ASD

Some autistic people will never even know themselves

Professionals are not always easily able to tell

In reality we don't really know how many people or how many women and girls have ASD

Statistics do however suggest that the number of women and girls with ASD is less than the number of men and boys with ASD. This could be because:

- Females are just less likely to have ASD genetically
- Females are under-diagnosed, compared to males
- Females do not 'show' their ASD as obviously
- Diagnostic criteria is based on males

We don't really know, these are just some hypotheses

What is a spectrum?

Autism is a 'spectrum' condition. It's sometimes depicted as a linear diagram, like this:

The Girl with the Curly Hair thinks this diagram may be a bit misleading. It suggests that an autistic person will be at a particular 'point' or 'end' of the spectrum

She thinks it might be better to think of the term spectrum to mean having different levels of ability and disability. Fundamentally, everyone is different!

'Functioning' is important to know about

An autistic person's ability to function (cope/'get by' in normal daily life) can fluctuate

There is sometimes an assumption that if an autistic person is coping fine and looks "normal", that they are like this all the time and that life must be "fine" for them

It's important to recognise that this ability to function is probably dependent on a number of factors and only when there are certain factors in place will a person be able to function well

These factors will be different for everyone but The Girl with the Curly Hair suspects that for most autistic people, they are:

Time spent alone and/or in their own space
Routines, rituals, structure
Special interests
Stimming/repetitive or restricted behaviours
Appropriate communication

If these factors are not in place, or aren't maintained for extended periods of time, perhaps a person's ability to cope will be significantly less and they may find life a lot more challenging

Also, don't underestimate the amount of effort an autistic person has to use in order to be just 'getting by'

I NEED AND ENJOY MY RITUALS, ROUTINES, STIMS STRUCTURE, MY OWN SPACE AND ENVIRONMENT AND MY SOLITUDE. WHEN PEOPLE TRY TO CHANGE OR STOP THOSE THINGS, I FEEL AS THOUGH THEY ARE TAKING AWAY THE THINGS THAT MAKE ME 'FUNCTION', MAKE ME HAPPY... AND THE THINGS THAT MAKE ME 'ME'

PEOPLE DON'T SEE THE UNDERLYING EFFORT THAT'S INVOLVED JUST DOING THE 'NORMAL TASKS' OF LIFE. NORMAL TASKS ARE OFTEN VERY DIFFICULT, VERY ANXIETY-PROVOKING AND VERY TIRING, EVEN IF THAT NEVER SHOWS ON THE SURFACE

ASD is a developmental disability, which means that an autistic person may have differences to their neurotypical peers in certain areas:

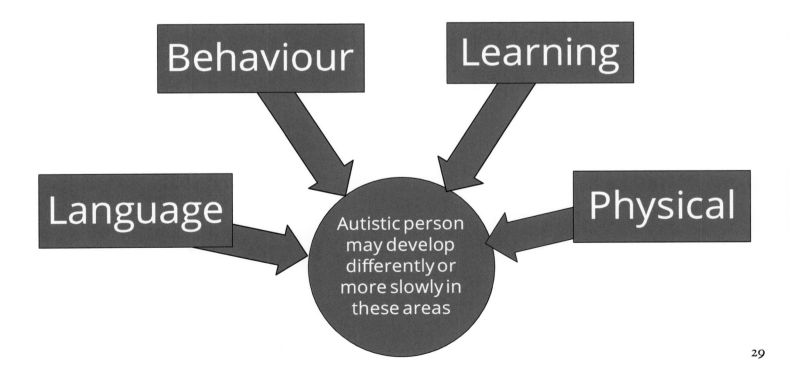

Behaviour

Learning

Language

Physical

Autistic person may develop differently or more slowly in these areas

Consequences of developmental disabilities:

Others	The Autistic Person
May need to support the autistic person more or for longer	May feel isolated and left out
May be more likely to take advantage, bully or harass	May feel 'different'
May need to be a bit more patient and understanding if the autistic person doesn't appear to yet be achieving potential	May struggle to connect with others of the same age
	May have low self-esteem due to finding life very hard or not reaching 'targets' despite really, really trying

The social impairments of ASD can mean an individual often feels as though they're living inside a glass jar:

Autistic people can have a lot of trouble making and/or keeping friends because their social impairments mean that they are likely to:

- Have different interests to others
- Have intense social anxiety
- Not understand social norms
- Need a lot of alone time
- Appear withdrawn, insensitive or unempathetic

Many of these things are because a person feels overwhelmed in situations and struggles to understand language, not because they don't want friends

Information processing

Another aspect of ASD to be aware of is that the way autistic people understand information is likely to be different. It's helpful to work out what works best for someone and try to incorporate that processing style into as many aspects of life as possible

The different ways that people understand things	
Alone	With other people
Being physically shown how to do something by someone else, being verbally taught by someone else	Reading something, looking at a visual, working something out by themselves
Talking	Writing things down
Quickly	Needing extra time
At a particular time of day	
In a particular environment	

Typical work or school environments might be very stressful for autistic people, who may require some adjustments in order to function properly

Sensory processing

Sensory processing is the way our brain and body respond to the stimulation around us, such as light, smell, sound and touch, etc.

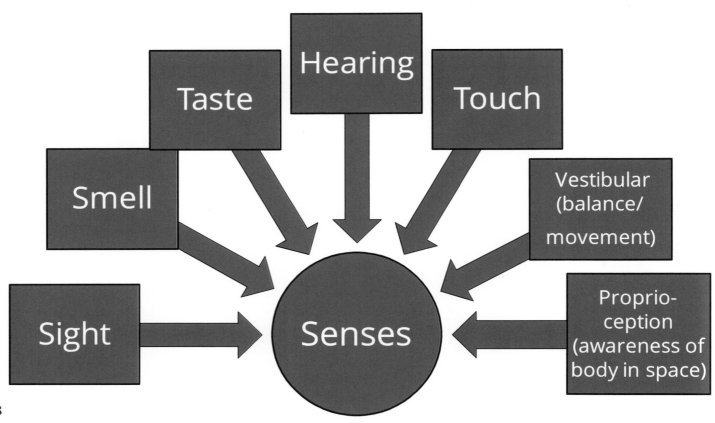

Another significant aspect to be aware of is that autistic individuals are very likely to have trouble with their sensory processing

It can mean having unusually intense experiences of sensations, such as finding sounds far too loud, colours too bright, smells too strong, etc. This is known as hypersensitivity

It can also mean having unusually unresponsive reactions to sensations, such as not being able to see things properly, not being able to smell, or needing very strong touch or pressure in order to 'feel' something. This is known as hyposensitivity

Considering how an animal such as a dog might receive and experience sensory experiences can help us have empathy for an autistic person who has difficulty with processing sensory information

Noisy upstairs neighbours

Reflections	

Bright coloured flowers blowing in the wind

Other animals' scents on wall

Wobbly pavement stone

Weather conditions

Dogs* can be hypersensitive to their environment and reactive to lots of sensations that most neurotypical people wouldn't really notice or be affected by

*Image inspired by Caring for Rescued ex Street Dogs
Caring for Rescued ex Street Dogs (2018.). In Facebook. Retrieved August 12, 2018 from http://www.facebook.com/caringforstreetdogs

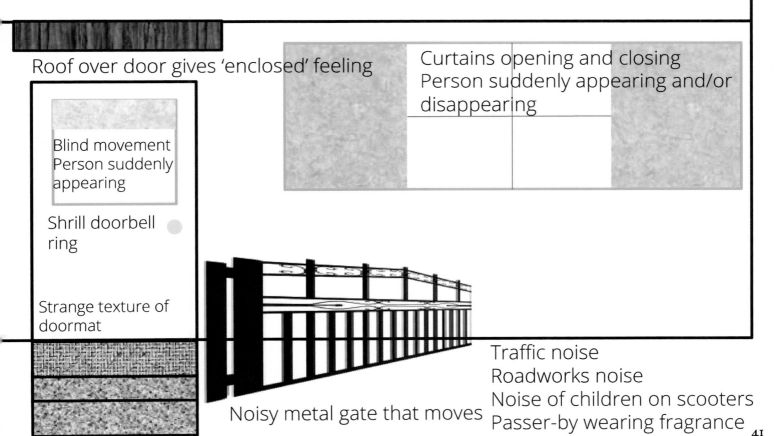

Children bouncing on trampoline next door
Dog barking next door

Roof over door gives 'enclosed' feeling

Curtains opening and closing
Person suddenly appearing and/or disappearing

Blind movement
Person suddenly appearing

Shrill doorbell ring

Strange texture of doormat

Traffic noise
Roadworks noise
Noise of children on scooters
Passer-by wearing fragrance or drinking coffee

Noisy metal gate that moves

Steps

Sensory processing has an impact on people's experience and enjoyment of normal life

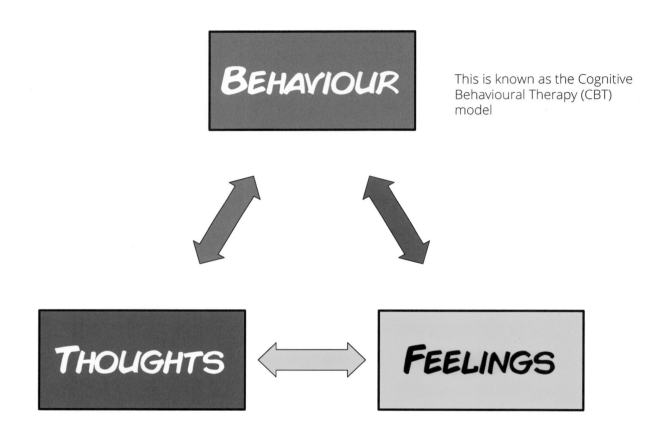

This is known as the Cognitive Behavioural Therapy (CBT) model

The way people feel affects the way they behave so if a person is feeling uncomfortable, anxious or overwhelmed, etc. because of their senses, it can show in their behaviour

Feelings	Uncomfortable, overwhelmed, too hot, too cold, in pain, terrified, anxious, etc.
Behaviours	Aggression, refusing to comply, 'strange' movements such as rocking, pacing, flapping, etc., being controlling, resisting direction, not wanting to do something, etc.

Personality types

There is a stereotype that all autistic people are introverted (which means they feel energised being on their own)

This is not true

Although lots of autistic people are introverted, many are extroverted (which means they feel energised being around other people)

Lots of autistic people appear introverted due to their difficulties, but they're actually extroverted!

Whether an autistic person is introverted or extroverted makes a big difference in how they present and behave!

ASD Extrovert

• Might be more obviously 'odd' or 'different'

• Might be considered annoying, loud and a bit "over the top"

• Likely to have clumsy social skills – talks too much or just about one topic

• Likely to crave new situations relating to their hobbies

• Likely to want to participate as much as possible

• May talk to anyone and everyone and know everyone by name!

both

• Might like to talk about their special interest
• Might find socialising hard
• Might have sensory processing difficulties
• Might get tired from socialising
• Might have repetitive or restricted behaviours and interests

ASD Introvert

• Likely to blend in more with the crowd and appear more 'normal'

• Might be seen as shy, withdrawn or aloof

• Likely to have clumsy social skills – may not speak a lot or not at all

• Likely to want to stay inside comfort zones of hobbies

• Likely to live life as an observer

• May keep themselves to themselves and in groups can easily be 'nobody's friend'

Social Energy Theory explains that different people have different capacities for socialising

Social energy is contained inside a tank and can go up and down:

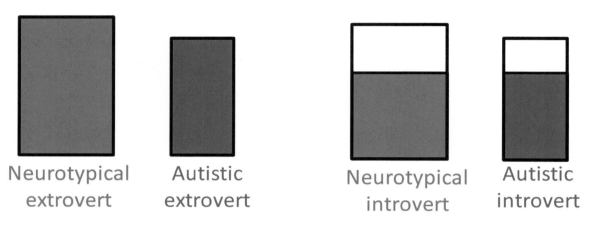

| Neurotypical extrovert | Autistic extrovert | Neurotypical introvert | Autistic introvert |

An extrovert's social energy goes up when they socialise; an introvert's social energy goes down when they socialise

When an introvert's tank is empty, they need recharge time; when an extrovert's tank is full, they need recharge time

As you can see however, social energy tanks of autistic people are smaller in size than the tanks of neurotypical people and they might not even be able to get full at all!

This is because socialising is difficult and anxiety-provoking due to the social impairments

The main consequence of this smaller capacity for social interactions is that autistic people - both extroverted and introverted - have less stamina for social situations and are likely to get tired more quickly

It's important to understand Social Energy Theory so that autistic people can learn to manage their energy better and adjust their lifestyle in order to keep their social energy inside the appropriate range for them

Co-occurring conditions

At least 40% of autistic people have anxiety at any time, compared with up to 15% in the general population*

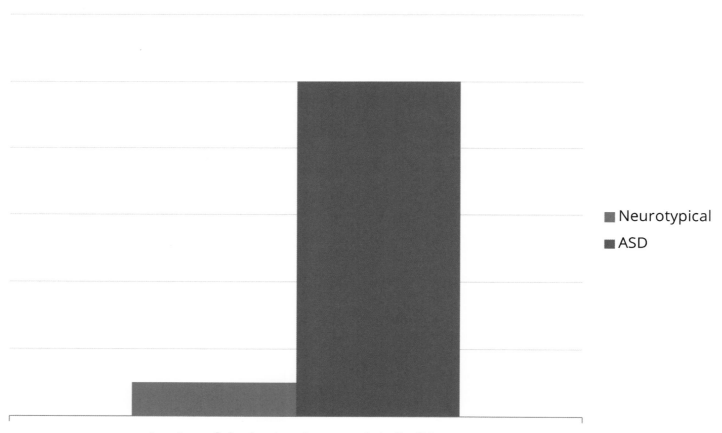

Anxiety felt during 'normal daily life'

Legend: Neurotypical, ASD

* National Autistic Society. 2018. Mental health and autism. [ONLINE] Available at: https://www.autism.org.uk/about/health/mental-health.aspx. [Accessed 11 August 2018].

A lot of neurotypical people don't realise that autistic people can have quite severe anxiety over things they didn't even think could cause anxiety

A lot of autistic people will be diagnosed with other conditions as well as ASD or before receiving an ASD diagnosis (this is because ASD can be easy to miss)

The table overleaf shows some of the similarities/overlap between ASD and other conditions, which highlights how there can be conflicting or different diagnoses depending on the clinician diagnosing

The Girl with the Curly Hair isn't sure that they're always separate diagnoses... she thinks that ASD is often at the core and may provide an explanation for many of these difficulties

Ultimately however, the label might not really matter - as long as the treatment the person receives works!

Common co-occurring problems	Relation to ASD
Eating disorders	• Someone who can't fit in might think that being thin will make them attractive and then they'll fit in • They might use food as a way to control some aspect of their life • Disordered eating can be due to sensory processing impairments • Person may struggle to recognise when they are full or when they are hungry due to weak interoception (ability of the brain to sense the internal state of the body)
Depression	• 'Shutdowns' could be seen as depression • Depression may occur due to social isolation, anxiety, social misunderstandings, etc.
OCD	• Repetitive behaviours
Social anxiety	• Social impairments can lead to social anxiety
ADHD	• Hypersensitivity • Person has difficulty concentrating • Person has excess energy due to being anxious
Dyspraxia	• Problems understanding verbal instructions • Problems with executive function • ASD is a developmental condition anyway

Diagnosis

A timely diagnosis of ASD may avoid many of the difficulties an individual experiences throughout their life and can also have many benefits and lead to a more positive lifestyle:

Some autistic people might not want a diagnosis and it's also important to be aware of the potential downsides:

People see the label, not the person
Stigma about ASD Solution: let people know what ASD is for <u>you</u>
People might very easily assume that ASD is the reason for any behaviour or traits a person has, instead of remembering that the person is still a human being!

Afraid or reluctant to admit you have a 'problem' or a 'disability'
It can be frightening to have confirmation that something is 'different' about you... or 'wrong' with you

People might treat you differently
People might change their behaviour around you (which is fine if that's what you want, but some people certainly won't want this to happen

These scenarios are examples of common problems The Girl with the Curly Hair encounters since obtaining her diagnosis

Some people seem to decide that ASD is the reason for everything and forget that underneath she is a person with her own personality together with likes and dislikes, just like everyone else (often nothing to do with ASD!)

So just be aware that once you have a label, people might begin to identify or 'use' that label to explain everything and overlook that you are still a human being with a unique personality...

Reasonable adjustments

ASD is a recognised disability which means the Equality Act 2010 applies

Organisations, services, education establishments and employers have a duty to make reasonable adjustments to ensure that autistic people aren't substantially disadvantaged

Reasonable adjustments are often straightforward

The Girl with the Curly Hair thinks that reasonable adjustments for autistic people can actually benefit neurotypical people too!

For example, lots of people can benefit from...

- Clear, concise, direct communication
  - Events running to time
    - Agendas in advance
    - Plans and structure
- Knowing about changes of plans in advance
  - Peaceful environments
  - Visual or written communication
  - Having undisturbed time

These are just a few examples of simple reasonable adjustments that can really make a huge difference to autistic people!

Summary

ASD causes people to have a different way of experiencing the world fundamentally based on two things: social and environment

ASD causes differences and difficulties in sensory processing together with the processing of information and communication

Autistic people might struggle with change and benefit from - or need - routines

Females with ASD often go misdiagnosed or are overlooked completely

Not every autistic person is introverted, some are extroverted

A diagnosis can be very important for many people because it helps them get the correct support. Some people need a diagnosis in order to fully be able to accept who they are (leading to significantly improved mental health)

ASD is a recognised disability – reasonable adjustments ought to be made (many of which are straightforward and can benefit everyone!)

Many thanks for reading

Other books in The Visual Guides series at the time of writing:

Asperger's Syndrome: Meltdowns and Shutdowns
Asperger's Syndrome Socialising & Social Energy
Asperger's Syndrome in 5-8 Year Olds
Asperger's Syndrome in 8-11 Year Olds
Asperger's Syndrome in 12-16 Year Old Girls
Asperger's Syndrome in 16-18 Year Olds
Asperger's Syndrome and Anxiety
Asperger's Syndrome: Helping Siblings
Asperger's Syndrome and Puberty
Asperger's Syndrome: Meltdowns and Shutdowns (2)
Adapting Health Therapies for People on the Autism Spectrum
Asperger's Syndrome and Emotions
Asperger's Syndrome and Communication
Asperger's Syndrome and Executive Function
Asperger's Syndrome: Understanding Each Other (For ASD/NT Couples)

New titles are continually being produced so keep an eye out!

Printed in Poland
by Amazon Fulfillment
Poland Sp. z o.o., Wrocław